At
the second
bus-stop
we see
a road sign.

The road sign
is like
a triangle.

At
the third
bus-stop
we see
a window.

The window
is like
a square.

At
the fourth
bus-stop
we see
a clock.

The clock
is like
a circle.

At
the fifth
bus-stop
we see
a ball.

The ball
is like
a sphere.

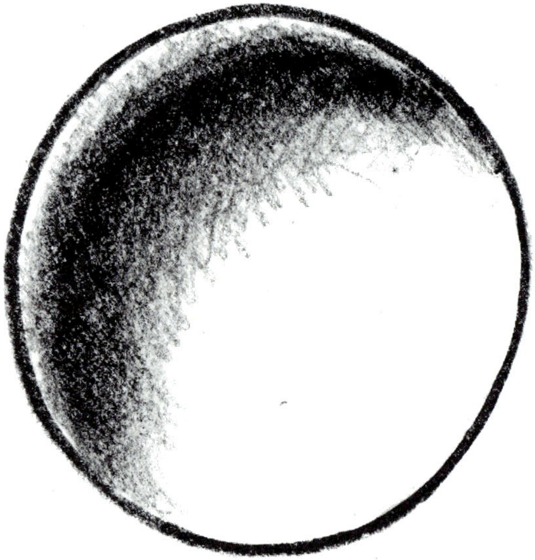

At
the sixth
bus-stop
we see
some bricks.

A brick
is like
a cuboid.

At
the seventh
bus-stop
we see
a roof.

The roof
is like
a pyramid.

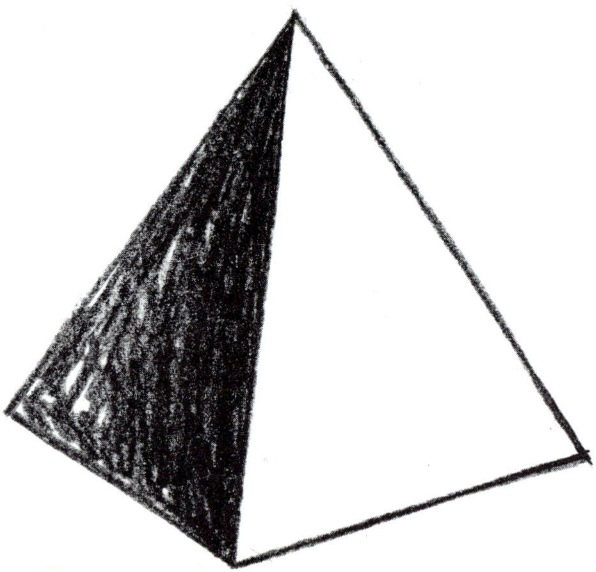

At
the eighth
bus-stop
we see
an ice-cream
cornet.

The ice-cream
cornet
is like
a cone.

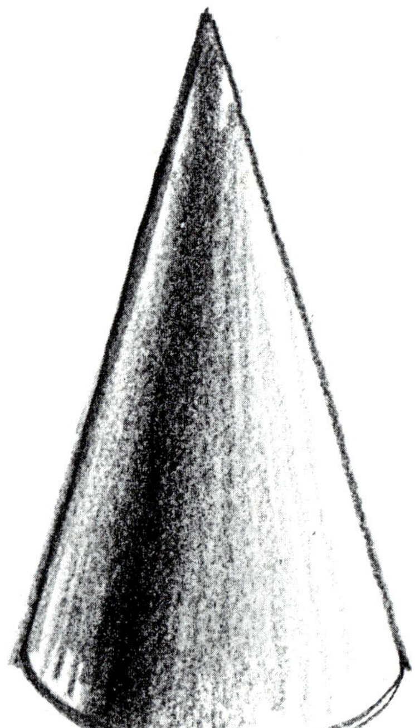

At
the ninth
bus-stop
we see
a drum.

The drum
is like
a cylinder.

At
the tenth
bus-stop
we see
a tent.

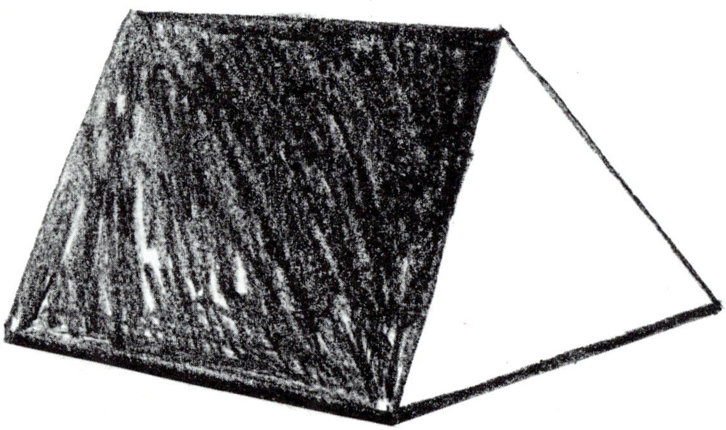

The tent
is like
a prism.

door  rectangle 

road sign  triangle 

window  square 

clock  circle 

ball  sphere 

brick  cuboid 

roof  pyramid 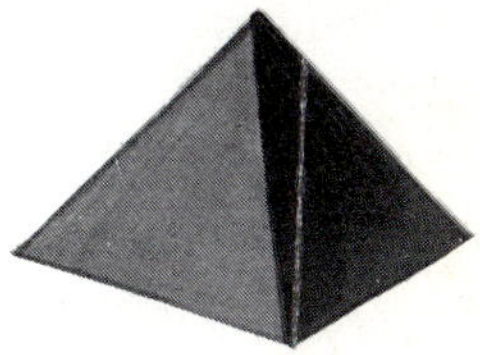

ice-cream cornet  cone 

drum  cylinder 

tent 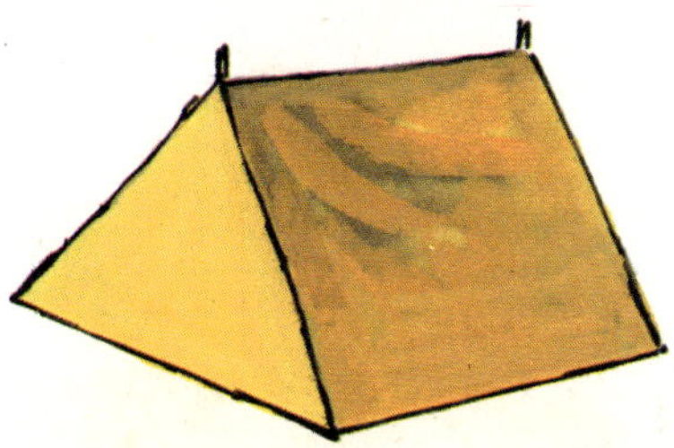 prism 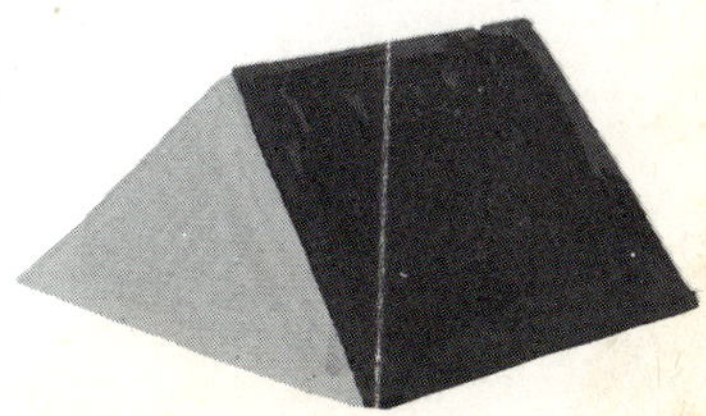

Ideas for Practical Work

Shapes are a part of everyday life, and children see them in this context. They should be given every opportunity to classify such shapes. This book illustrates the more common shapes we see around us. A tour of the local environment which involves discussion and questions about shapes will further the work that has been initiated here.

The shapes referred to in the book are big and static, and to help children appreciate the properties of shape it is useful to have objects they can handle. A collection of empty containers, such as washing powder packets, chocolate boxes, etc., is useful for a sorting exercise. The children can be given a large number of these boxes and be asked to sort them. They should be asked to put them into their own categories, such as those with "flat faces" and those with "round faces". This work can lead to a discussion about both two-dimensional and three-dimensional shapes. The children will learn the properties of these shapes whilst they play with them and explore them with their hands. With the help of discussion they will see that a cuboid has six faces, which are rectangles, twelve edges, and eight vertices; they will also learn that a cube is a "special" cuboid which has squares for all its faces.

In order that the children may see a net of a shape, a box can be carefully cut along its edges and opened out flat. They can then try making their own shape using a net they have drawn on card. They can also make shapes out of clay or similar media. They can use these, and other boxes, to make models such as houses, churches, railway engines, motor cars, etc.

Young children will come to learn the properties of shape through practical work accompanied by discussion with the teacher, so it is important to make sure that these opportunities are frequently available to them.

PATTERNS we see from the Big Red Bus

At
the first
bus-stop
we see
a wall.
The wall
has a pattern.

The pattern
is made
of rectangles.

At
the second
bus-stop
we see windows.
The windows
have a pattern.

The pattern
is made
of rectangles.

RITZ
HOTEL

At
the third
bus-stop
we see
another wall.
The wall
has a pattern.

The pattern
is made
of squares.

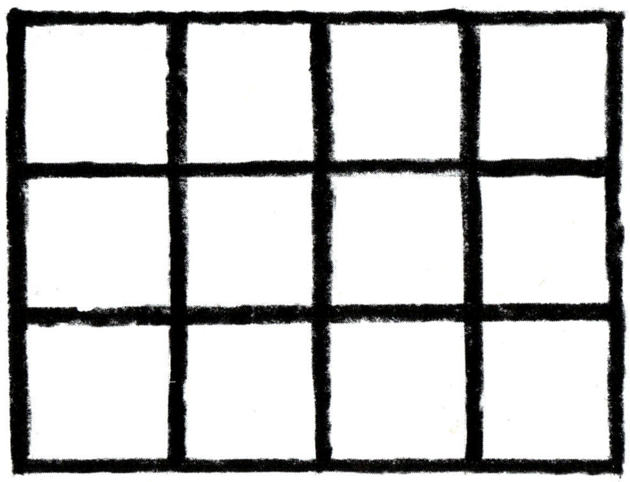

At
the fourth
bus-stop
we see
a fence.
The fence
has a pattern.

The pattern
is made
of squares.

At
the fifth
bus-stop
we see
a bridge.
The bridge
has a pattern.

The pattern
is made
of triangles.

At
the sixth
bus-stop
we see
a big wheel.
The big wheel
has a pattern.

The pattern
is made
of triangles.

At
the seventh
bus-stop
we see
lights on a car.
The lights
have a pattern.

The pattern
is made
of circles.

10
38

At
the eighth
bus-stop
we see
a target.
The target
has a pattern.

The pattern
is made
of circles.

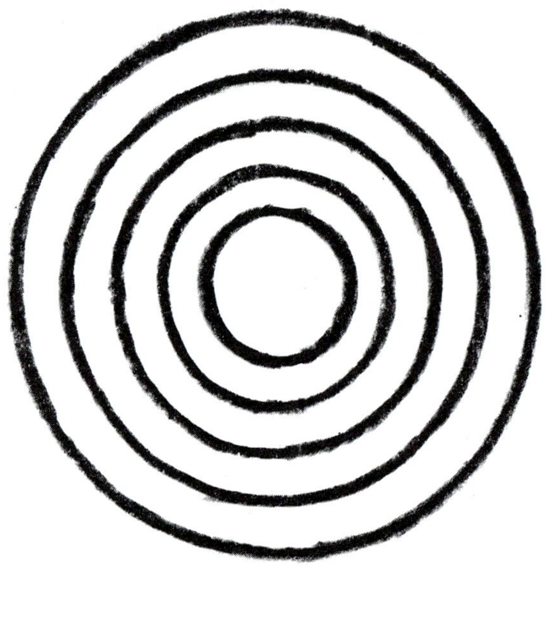

At
the ninth
bus-stop
we see
a stack of tins.
The stack
has a pattern.

The pattern
is made
of cylinders.

At
the tenth
bus-stop
we see
a pile of boxes.
The pile
has a pattern.

The pattern
is made
of cuboids.

wall  rectangle pattern

windows  rectangle pattern

wall 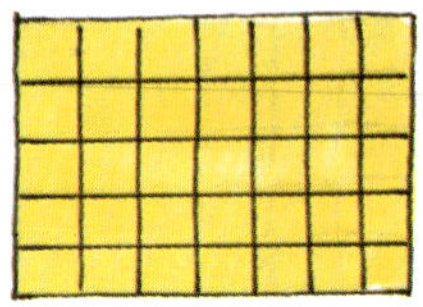 square pattern

fence 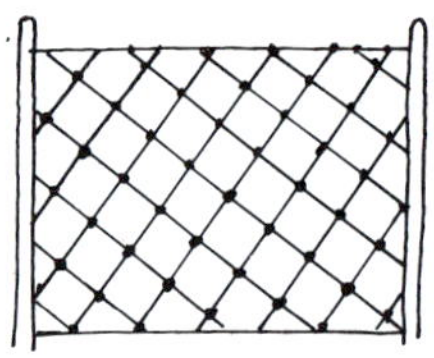 square pattern

bridge  triangle pattern

big wheel 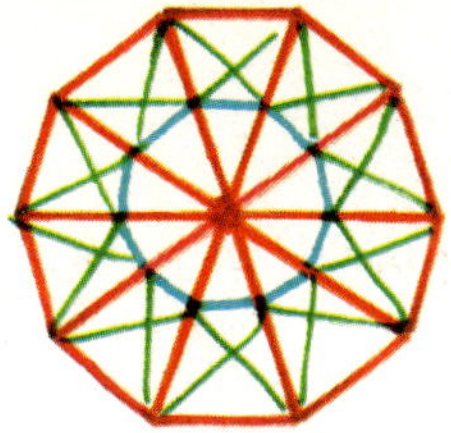 triangle pattern

lights  circle pattern

target 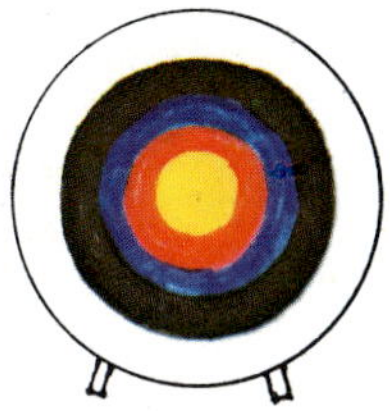 circle pattern

tins  cylinder pattern

boxes  cuboid pattern

Ideas for Practical Work

Children are able to appreciate some of the properties of shapes by observing the different pattern arrangements that can be made with them. Thus they will notice that rectangles make a pattern that can completely fill an area (an idea that leads to tessellations). They may also notice that squares behave in the same way. With discussion this can lead to the conclusion that a square is a "special" rectangle. Patterns with circles are more difficult, because they will leave gaps when they are fitted together.

This book initiates the idea of pattern by illustrating pattern arrangements for several shapes. Children should be encouraged to see if they can find different patterns from those which are shown in the book. Two-dimensional patterns can be made with coloured sticky paper, shapes or tiles, and three-dimensional patterns with old boxes, packets or playing bricks.

Encouragement should be given to the children to experiment and discuss their work. Experimentation allows them to see those ideas of pattern which will not work, as well as those which do; consequently helping them to appreciate the properties of pattern and shape.

COMPARE with us

from the Big Red Bus

At
the first
bus-stop
we see
two trains.

One train
is long,
one train
is short.

We see four wagons...

This wagon
is the
longest.

This wagon
is the
shortest.

At
the second
bus-stop
we see two cars.

One car
is large,
one car
is small.

We see three boxes...

This box
is the
largest.

This box
is the
smallest.

At .
the third
bus-stop
we see
two ropes.

One rope is thick,
one rope is thin.

We see five planks...

This plank
is the
thickest.

This plank
is the
thinnest.

At
the fourth
bus-stop
we see
two doors.

One door
one door

is wide,
is narrow.

We see six brushes...

This brush
is the
widest.

This brush
is the
narrowest.

At
the fifth
bus-stop
we see
two teachers.

One teacher is tall,
one teacher is short.

We see seven children...

This child
is the
tallest.

This child
is the
shortest.

long

large

thick

wide

tall

short

small

thin

narrow

short

Ideas for Practical Work

Comparison is a prerequisite for measurement, and to become well acquainted with this aspect of mathematics children need plenty of practical activities. Such activities arise in everyday life, where comparisons are made as a matter of course, but this can only be enhanced if children are encouraged to discuss their observations. If two children have painted trains, we would expect them to make comments such as: "This is the shortest train", "This train has a long engine", "My train is longer than your train". Comments like these reinforce the concept of comparison.

Most of the follow-up work for this book will arise from observing the environment and making comparisons. A walk along a street gives the teacher opportunities to ask such questions as "Can you show me a tall building?" and "Can you see a small car?" It is expected that comparisons other than those in the book will be used, e.g. heavy, light; such ideas can be best understood by children actually feeling the heaviness and lightness of objects.

A further extension of the book would be to introduce the idea of "the same length", the same width", etc., which will prepare the children for work on measurement.

MEASURE with us from the Big Red Bus

At
the first
bus-stop
we see
a hedge.

The hedge is
one man high.

At
the second
bus-stop
we see
a wall.

The wall is
two men high.

At
the third
bus-stop
we see
a car.

The car is
two ladies wide.

At
the fourth
bus-stop
we see
a doorway.

The doorway is
three ladies wide.

At
the fifth
bus-stop
we see
a van.

The van is
one ladder long.

At
the sixth
bus-stop
we see
a lorry.

The lorry is
three ladders long.

At
the seventh
bus-stop
we see
a carpet.

The carpet is
one stride wide.

At
the eighth
bus-stop
we see
a bridge.

The bridge is
eight strides wide.

At
the ninth
bus-stop
we see
some boxes.

One of the boxes is
one metre high.

At
the tenth
bus-stop
we see
a cupboard.

The cupboard is
two metres high.

hedge  one man high

wall  two men high

car  two ladies wide

doorway  three ladies wide

van  one ladder long lorry  three ladders long

carpet  one stride wide

bridge  eight strides wide

box  one metre high

cupboard  two metres high

Ideas for Practical Work

In this book we take the idea of comparison (as in *Compare with us from the Big Red Bus*) a step further. The child now needs to observe equality in order to measure. Looking at the book the child sees a hedge with a man by the side of it. He observes that they are the same height, and learns that "the hedge is one man high" implies that the hedge is the same height as the man. In this book the measurements are arbitrary, so in the case of the hedge the unit is the man. The child should be encouraged to use a variety of unit measures, even if some turn out to be unconventional or inappropriate. A desk may be "four books long" or "three dolls high"– there are endless possibilities for measuring with non-standard measures.

As a progression the child should use body measures which include strides, arms' lengths, spans, and hand widths. By using such body measurements and comparing results with other children, the child learns that these are not good units, as they tend to vary from child to child.

If metre rules are left in the room, some children may use them as a method of measuring longer distances: "the room is seven rulers long", "the hall is ten rulers wide". The teacher can use this opportunity to show the children that the rulers are all the same length, and that this length is called a metre. Instead of saying "The room is seven rulers long", the child learns to say, "The room is seven metres long".

Children should be expected to measure as many things as possible over a period of time. It is through practical work that they are more able to achieve the best concept of measurement.

SETS we see from the Big Red Bus

At
the first
bus-stop
we see
some fishermen.

They make
a set
of fishermen.

At
the third
bus-stop
we see
a set of cleaners.

All the cleaners
make the set.

At
the fourth
bus-stop
we see
a set of cats.

There are
three members
of the set of cats.

At
the fifth
bus-stop
we see
a set of musicians.

There are
six members
of the set of musicians.

At
the seventh
bus-stop
we see
a set of ladies.

The ladies
with hats
are two members
of the set of ladies.

At
the eighth
bus-stop
we see
a set of children.

The four girls
are members
of the set of children.

At
the ninth
bus-stop
we look for
a set of sailors.

There is
one member
of the set of sailors.

At
the tenth
bus-stop
we look for
a set of workmen.

There are
no workmen.
It is an empty set.